Speech To The Youth

Speech To The Youth

Jean Jaurès

Translated by
Will Johncock
Foreword by
Gilles Candar

Planktos Press

Published by Planktos Press.
Sydney, Australia.
www.planktospress.com

Paperback ISBN: 978-1-922931-06-1
eBook ISBN: 978-1-922931-07-8

Speech To The Youth was originally published in French under the titles *Discours à la jeunesse (1903)*, by chez Cornély, Paris, and *Discours de Jaurès (1903)*, by La Petite République Socialiste, Paris.

Contents

Foreword   i

Speech To The Youth   1

This is undoubtedly the best-known text, or at least the most often cited, of Jean Jaurès (1859-1914). An orator of great talent, a tireless and subtle politician, a humanist, scholar, philosopher, historian and journalist, Jaurès was, and in a certain way is increasingly becoming, the key reference in France not only for socialism, but for the whole of the French left, and indeed for the Republic and democracy in general. Today, passages from this speech on the meaning of history, the fight for peace, and above all his beautiful definition of courage as the supreme hope of human life, adorn – and will probably continue to adorn for a long time – many political, academic, professional, and other speeches.

Yet this was not the case during Jaurès' lifetime. Admittedly, the speech was noticed, and received some attention, at the time, but people quickly moved on to other things in the heat of the summer. Let's look at the circumstances. It was 30

July 1903. Jaurès was invited to deliver the customary speech at the prize-giving ceremony at the lycée d'Albi (Albi secondary school). He knew the school well. He himself had been a pupil at the college in Castres, in the south of the same French department of Tarn, before continuing his studies in Paris. But after completing the agrégation in 1881 (the highest teaching diploma in France), he was appointed professor at the lycée d'Albi, where he remained for two years. He then moved to Toulouse, the regional capital, to teach at the University, before embarking on a political career. He had given the speech in 1883 as a young teacher, in 1888 while he was a Republican member of parliament for Tarn, and he made it again in 1903. Indeed, he had become a socialist, having fought in a lot of political and social struggles, but by 1903, the Bloc des gauches (Lefts Block), which he supported, were exercising power. He was then vice-president of the Chambre des députés (Chamber of the

Members of Parliament) for a year, and supported the anti-clerical action of the Combes government (1902-1905) which led to *La loi de séparation des Églises et de l'État* (Law on the separation of the Churches and the State) (9 December 1905). This all explains the invitation extended to him by his former lycée to give this speech. Neither the minister, nor the academic authorities, could object to this.

His speech was published in brochure form by a Parisian publisher, Cornély, and reprinted by the Paris daily newspaper with which Jaurès was associated at the time, *La Petite République*, in its 2 August 1903 edition. However, by definition, if the daily newspaper was read at the time, current events soon made the speech quickly forgotten, and the brochure itself, whose print run was probably modest and in the order of a few hundred copies, quickly sold out. Attention was on new events: high profile court cases, social struggles, attempts to revive the Dreyfus affair in order to officially prove that the unjustly convicted captain is innocent, a disaster on the Paris metro, conflicts between Catholics and anticlericals over religious congregations, the Italian royal couple's trip to France, etc. Neither *L'Humanité*, the new newspaper founded by Jaurès in April 1904, nor the Socialist Party, unified in 1905 and of which Jaurès quickly became the prestigious leader, nor anyone else, thought to speak again about this speech or to reprint it.

Jaurès was assassinated on 31 July 1914, on the eve of the Great War, by a weak-minded person, who feared Jaurès' actions. During the war, Jaurès' fight for peace was sometimes mentioned and his speech of 1903 was quoted, here or there, in the press or at conferences. But it was not until the 1920s that the speech was again heard and known. This happened in 1927 with the recording of excerpts from the speech (the conclusion on the topic of courage), read by an actress, Suzanne Desprès, in the rather grandiloquent tone then in fashion. The publication of the speech in brochure form by the Socialist Party in 1929 was also especially effective in the speech becoming known again. This new publication was a huge success and from then on was followed by many different reprints and re-editions during the 1930s, then after the war, in the 1950s, the 1970s, and up to the present day.

We hope that this text will interest and touch the Australian public. It is aimed at young people who were among the generations most directly exposed to the massacres of the Great War. This was to be the case of Louis, the son of Jean Jaurès, who volunteered and was killed during the German offensives of 1918, before even having reached his 20th birthday. In fact, it deals with all topics, it is a general reflection on the meaning of life and the direction that Jaurès chose, in terms that are clear, eloquent, and accessible to a wide audience.

The political and social situation in Australia was little known at the time to the French public. It was however mentioned from time to time in the French press. Among the socialists, it is necessary to mention at least two names who were great couriers of culture and experience, and informants of the first order. Jean Longuet (1876-1938), a grandson of Karl Marx, who was to play a major role in socialist pacifism and the anthem *l'Internationale*, was an editor at *L'Humanité* after having worked at *La Petite République*, and was particularly specialised in English speaking countries, since he spoke and wrote English fluently. He was born in London, during the exile of his father, a former member of the Paris Commune, and had subsequently maintained and developed his language skills and knowledge of the vast English-speaking world, becoming a specialist in international issues. He gathered information, read the press and books, and had links with many socialist leaders around the entire world since his birth.

The other expert regarding Australia was in a slightly different situation. Albert Métin (1871-1918) was a brilliant student, a pupil of prestigious schools (École Normale Supérieure, Hautes Études Commerciales, École Coloniale, Conservatoire national des arts et métiers), and finally of the teaching "agrégation" in history and geography. Of libertarian sensibilities, to the left of socialism, he benefited from being awarded an Albert Kahn grant to travel around the world for eighteen months. He visited in particular Australia and New Zealand from 27 April to 3 October 1899. Upon returning, he published a book: *Le socialisme sans doctrines. La question agraire et la question ouvrière en Australie et en Nouvelle-Zélande* (Paris, Alcan, 1901; Translated into English as *Socialism without Doctrines*, Chippendale, Alternative Publishing Co-operative, 1977). Métin became a moderate socialist, outside the unified party. In 1906 he managed the cabinet of the first socialist minister for labour, René Viviani, who also broke with the party. He was then elected as a Radical-Socialiste party minister for Doubs and during the war began a ministerial career, with La gauche républicaine (The Republican Left), but he died prematurely at the of 47.

Jean Longuet remained a member of Jaurès' Socialist Party. He provides an account of the progress of the Australian Labor Party, in particular regarding the first governments led by Andrew Fisher (1862-1928). He praises their success, while regretting their protectionist tendencies and nationalist prejudices, a debate that was destined to happen again. He counted however on the future, and welcomed the Labor Party's decision to join the Socialist International organisation before the planned conference in 1914 in Vienna. In May 1913, during Andrew Fisher's European tour, he and Ramsay

MacDonald were asked to organise a meeting between the Australian Prime Minister and Jean Jaurès, about which we unfortunately know nothing, at least in France.

In a way, Métin represents the political left of reality, pragmatic and modest, while Longuet wants to maintain principles, his approach is obviously more ideological, more inspired by Marxism. Jean Jaurès represents and surpasses them both, wishing "to go for the ideal and to understand the real". Let's hope that this publication will help aid a mutual understanding, and will be a useful contribution to cultural relations, between France and Australia.

Gilles Candar
Président de la Société d'études jaurésiennes
21 November 2023
(Translated by Will Johncock)

Ladies, gentlemen, young students.

It's a great joy for me to be back at this school in Albi and to speak again for a moment. A great joy, tinged with a little melancholy, because when you only come back at long intervals, you suddenly realise what the indifferent flight of days has taken from us and given to the past. Time had robbed us of ourselves, parcel by parcel, and all of a sudden we see that a big block of our life is far away from us. The long anthill of minutes, each carrying a grain, passes silently, until one beautiful evening the barn is empty.

But does it matter that time takes away our strength little by little, if it uses it obscurely for vast works in which something of us survives? Twenty-two years ago, it was I who delivered the customary speech. I remember (and perhaps one of my colleagues from then also remembers) that I had chosen as the theme: human judgements. I asked those who were listening to me to judge men with benevolence, that is to say, with fairness, to be attentive even to the most mediocre minds and the most destitute existences, to the features of light, to the fleeting sparks of moral beauty through which human nature's vocation for greatness is revealed. I begged them to interpret with leniency the groping effort of an uncertain humanity.

Perhaps in the years of struggle that followed, I failed more than once to apply this advice of generous fairness towards my opponents. What reassures me a little is that I imagine they must have sometimes failed regarding me also, and that restores the balance. What remains true, through all our miseries, through all the injustices committed or suffered, is that it is necessary to give wide credit to human nature. It is that we condemn ourselves to not understanding humanity, if we do not have a sense of its greatness and an intuition of its incomparable destinies.

This belief is not foolish, blind, nor frivolous. It does not ignore the vices, crimes, errors, prejudices, egoisms of all kinds, the selfishness of individuals, castes, parties, and classes, which weigh down the progress of mankind, and often absorb the course of the river in a murky and bloody whirlpool. It knows that the forces of good and wisdom, light and justice, cannot occur without the help of time, and that the night of servitude and ignorance is not dispelled by a sudden and total illumination, but alleviated only by a slow series of uncertain dawns.

Yes, men who have trust in mankind know this. They are resigned in advance to only seeing an incomplete realisation of their vast ideal, which itself will be surpassed, or rather, they welcome that all human possibilities do not manifest within the narrow limits of their lives. They are full of a deferential and painful sympathy for those who, having been brutalised by immediate experience, have conceived bitter thoughts, as well as for those whose lives have coincided with periods of servitude, debasement and reaction, and who, under the dark, motionless cloud, might have believed that the day would never dawn again. But they themselves are very careful to not write off the misfortunes of passing generations as a liability of a humanity that endures. And they affirm, with unwavering certainty, that it is worth the trouble of thinking and acting, that human effort toward clarity and justice is never lost. History teaches us the difficulty of great tasks and the slowness of accomplishments, but it also justifies invincible hope.

In our modern France, what therefore is the Republic? It is a great act of confidence. To institute the Republic is to proclaim that millions of men will themselves know how to draw up the common rule of their action; that they will know to how to reconcile liberty and law, movement and order; that they will know how to fight each other without tearing each other apart; that their divisions will not go as far as the chronic fury of civil war, and; that they will never seek in a temporary dictatorship a dreadful truce and a cowardly rest. To institute the Republic, is to proclaim that the citizens of the great modern nations, bound by constant work for the necessities of private and domestic life, will nevertheless have enough time and freedom of mind to concern themselves with the common good. And if this Republic arises suddenly in a still monarchical world, it is to ensure that it will adapt to the complicated conditions of international life, without engaging in the slower evolution of other peoples, but also without abandoning anything of its just pride and, without dimming the brilliance of its principle.

Yes, the Republic is a great act of belief and a great act of daring. Its invention was so audacious, so paradoxical, that even the bold men who, one hundred and ten years ago, revolutionised the world, initially dismissed the idea of it. The constituents of 1789 and 1791, even the legislators of 1792, believed that the traditional monarchy was the necessary envelope for the new society. They only renounced this shelter under the repeated blows of royal treason. And when finally they had uprooted royalty, the Republic appeared to them less like a predestined system than as the only means of filling the void left by the monarchy. Soon, however, after a few hours of amazement and almost anxiety, they adopted it with all their minds and hearts. They summed up, they mixed up, the entire Revolution in it. And they did not seek to fool each other. They did not look to reassure themselves by the example of the ancient republics or the Helvetic or Italian republics. The saw that they were creating a new work, bold and without precedent. This was not the oligarchic freedom of the republics of Greece, broken up, tiny and based on slave labour. It was not the superb privilege of serving the Roman republic, the lofty citadel from which a conquering aristocracy dominated the world, communicating with it through a hierarchy of incomplete and diminishing rights that descended to the nothingness of law, via a staircase of ever more degraded and dark steps, which finally lost itself in the abjectness of slavery, the obscure limit of life touching the subterranean night. This was not the patriciate merchant of Venice and Genoa. No, this was the Republic of a great people, where there were only citizens and where all citizens were equal. It was the Republic of democracy and universal suffrage. It was a magnificent and moving novelty.

The men of the Revolution were aware of this. And when, in the party of 10 August 1793, they celebrated this Constitution, which for the first time since the dawn of history, organised national sovereignty and the sovereignty of all, when artisans and workers, blacksmiths, carpenters and field workers marched in procession, mingled with the magistrates of the people and brandished their tools, the President of the Convention was able to say that it was a day like no other, the most beautiful day since the sun was suspended in the immensity of space. All wills drew themselves up to the measure of this heroic novelty. It was, for her, that these men fought and died. It was in its name that they forced back the kings of Europe. It was in its name that they decimated themselves. And they concentrated in it a life so ardent and terrible, they produced through it so many acts and thoughts, that one could believe that this brand-new Republic, without model and likewise without traditions, had acquired in a few years the strength and substance of centuries. And yet there were vicissitudes and tests before this Republic, which the men of the Revolution had believed to be imperishable, was finally founded on our soil. Not only was it defeated after a few stormy years, but it seems that it disappeared forever from history as well as from the very memory of mankind. It was ridiculed, outraged; more than that, it was forgotten. For half a century, except for a few deep hearts that kept hold of the memory and the hope, men disowned or even ignored her. The supporters of the old regime only speak of it in order to shame the Revolution: "This is where revolutionary delirium has led". And among those who profess to defend the modern world, to continue the tradition of the Revolution, most disavow the Republic and democracy. It's as if they no longer even remember it. Guizot exclaims: "Universal suffrage will never have its day". As if it had not already had its great days in history, as if the Convention had not come out of it. Theirs, when he recounts the revolution of 10 August, neglects to mention that it proclaimed universal suffrage, as if that was an unimportant accident and an odd quirk just of one day. The Republic, universal suffrage, democracy, these were, according to the wise, the feverish dreams of the men of the Revolution. Their work remains, but their fever is extinguished, and the modern world that they founded, if it is bound to continue their work, is not bound to continue their delirium. The abrupt resurrection of the Republic, reappearing in 1848 only to vanish in 1851, indeed seemed like a brief relapse into a nightmare soon to dissipate.

And so it is now that this Republic, which so greatly surpassed the age-old experience of men and the common level of thought that when it fell its very ruins perished and its memory crumbled, that this Republic of democracy, of universal suffrage and of universal human dignity, which had not had a model and which seemed destined to have no tomorrow, has become the enduring law of the nation, the definitive form of French life, the type towards which all the democracies of the world are slowly progressing.

Now, and this is what I especially want to

point out to you, the very audacity of the attempt contributed to its success. The idea of a great people governing itself was so noble, that in times of difficulty and crisis, it offered itself to the conscience of the nation. The first time in 1793 the people of France had climbed to this summit, and there tasted such pride, underneath the apparent oversight and indifference, the need to rediscover this extraordinary emotion remained. What made the force of the Republic invincible was that it did not simply appear from period to period, in the disaster or disarray of other regimes, as the necessary expedient and forced solution. It was a consolation and a pride. It alone had enough moral nobility to give the nation the strength to forget disappointments and to overcome disasters. That is why it had to have the last word. Many are the slips and many are the falls on the escarpments which lead to the summits, but the summits have an attractive force. The Republic has won because it is in the direction of the heights, and man cannot rise without climbing towards it. The law of gravity does not act supremely over human societies, and it is not in low places that they find their equilibrium. Those who, for a century, have set their ideal very high, have been justified by history. And those who set it even higher will also be justified. For the proletariat in general is beginning to assert that it is not only in the political relations of men, but also in their economic and social relations, that it is necessary to introduce true freedom, equality, and justice. It is not only the city, it is the workshop, it is work, it is production, it is the property that he wants to organise according to the republican example. He intends to replace a system that divides and oppresses, with a vast social cooperation in which all the workers of all kinds, workers of the hand and workers of the brain, under the direction of leaders freely elected by them, will administer production that is finally organised.

Gentleman, I am not forgetting that I alone

have the floor and that this privilege commands much stock in me. I will not abuse this privilege in order to draw up an idea for this festival around which battles are being fought and will continue to be fought. But how would it be possible for me to speak to this youth, who is the future, without letting my thoughts out about the future? I would have offended you by being too cautious about this, for whatever your feelings about the bottom of things, you are all spirits that are too free to ever reproach me for having affirmed here this high socialist hope, which is the light of my life. I only want to say two things, for they touch not on the basic problem, but on the method of the mind and the conduct of the thought. Firstly, you have the right to be demanding towards a bold idea that is set to shake up and weaken so many interests and habits and which claims to renew the very basis of life. You have the right to ask it to prove itself, that is to say, to establish precisely how it relates to all political and social evolution, and how it can fit into it. You have the right to ask by which set of legal and economic forms it will ensure the transition from the existing to the new order. You have the right to demand that the first applications that can be made of it add to the economic and moral vitality of the nation. And it must prove, in showing itself to be capable of defending what is already noble and good in the human heritage, that it is not about to waste it, but to enlarge it. It would have little faith in itself if it did not accept these conditions.

You, on the other hand, you owe it to study it with a free mind, which is not troubled by any class interest. You owe it to not oppose it with frivolous mockeries, those blind or premeditated panics, and that bias of ironic or brutal negation that so often, for a century, is even how the wise have opposed the Republic, which is now accepted by all, at least in its form. And if you are still tempted to say that we must not linger, to study or to discuss dreams, look at one of your suburbs. What mockery, what sinister prophecies about the work that is there! What gloomy prognoses against the workers who intended to find their way themselves, to try out in a large industry the form of collective ownership of property and the virtue of free discipline. The work has endured however, it has grown, it allows us to glimpse what collectivist cooperation can produce. A humble bud, definitely, but one that is a testament to the work of the sap, the slow rise of new ideas, and the transformative power of life. Nothing lies more than the old pessimistic and reactionary adage of the disillusioned Ecclesiastes: "There is nothing new under the sun". The sun itself even was once a novelty, and the earth was a novelty, and man was a novelty. Human history is only a ceaseless effort of invention, and perpetual evolution is perpetual creation.

It is therefore with a free spirit also that you will welcome this other great novelty which is announcing itself with multiplied symptoms: lasting peace between nations, definitive peace. This is not to dishonour the war in the past. It has been a part of great human action, and man has ennobled it through thought and courage, through exalted heroism, through magnanimous contempt for death. For a long time in the chaos of a disordered humanity that is saturated with brutal instincts, it has been without doubt the only means of resolving conflicts. It has also been the harsh force which, in pitting tribes, peoples, and races against each other, mixed human elements and lay the foundation for vast groupings. But the day is coming, and everything tells us that it is near, when humanity is organised enough, and enough a master of itself, to be able to resolve the conflicts between its groups and forces by reason, negotiation, and law. And war, detestable and great while it was necessary, is atrocious and villainous when it begins to seem unnecessary.

I am not proposing to you an idyllic and

vain dream. For too long, the ideas of peace and human unity have been nothing more than a high, illusory brightness, that ironically shed light on the ongoing killings. Do you remember the admirable depiction left to us by Virgil of the fall of Troy? It is night, the surprised city is invaded by iron and flames, by murder, fire, and despair. Priam's palace is forced open and the doors knocked down to reveal the long row of apartments and galleries. From room to room, torches and swords pursue the vanquished. Children, women, and the elderly, take refuge in vain at the domestic alter, that the sacred laurel no longer protects against death and outrage. Blood flows in gushes and every mouth cries out in terror, pain, insult, and hatred. But over the stricken, screaming residence, the inner courtyards, the collapsed roofs allow a glimpse of the great, serene, and peaceful sky, and all the human clamour of violence and agony rises towards the golden stars: Ferit aurea sidera clamor.

Likewise, for twenty centuries, and from period to period, every time a star of unity and peace has risen over mankind, the torn and dark earth has responded with clamours of war.

At first it was the imperious star of conquering Rome which believed to have absorbed all the conflicts in the universal radiance of its force. The empire collapsed under the impact of the barbarians, and a horrifying tumult responded to the superb pretention of Roman peace. Then it was the Christian star, which enveloped the earth in a glow of tenderness and promise of peace. But although soft and gentle on the Galilean horizons, it rose, dominating and harsh over feudal Europe. The claim of the Papacy to calm the world under its law and in the name of Catholic unity only added to the troubles and conflicts of miserable humanity. The convulsions and murders of nations of the Middle Ages, the bloody clashes of modern nations, were the derisory retort to the grand promise of

Christian peace. The Revolution, in turn, raises a high signal of universal peace through universal liberty. And there we are, from the very struggle of the Revolution against the forces of the old world, formidable wars are developing.

What? Peace will always escape us? And the clamour of men, always frenzied and disappointed, will continue to rise towards the golden stars from modern capitals set on fire by shells, as from the ancient palace of Praim that was burned down by torches? No! No! Despite the prudent and cautious advice that these grandiose disappointments give us, I dare say, with millions of men, that now the great human peace is possible, and if we want it, it is near. New forces are at work: democracy, methodological science, the universal, united proletariat. War is becoming more difficult because, with free governments and modern democracies, it is becoming at once both the peril of all through universal service and the crime of all through universal suffrage. War is becoming more difficult because science envelops all people in a multiplied network, in a fabric of relations, exchanges, and conventions that gets tighter daily, and if the first effect of discoveries that abolish distances is sometimes to aggravate friction, in the long run they create a solidarity, a human familiarity that makes war a monstrous attack and a kind of collective suicide.

Finally, the common ideal that exalts and unites the proletarians of all countries, makes them more resistant to the intoxication of war, to the hatred and rivalries between nations and races. Yes, as history has given the last word to the Republic, so often ridiculed and trampled, so it will give the last word to peace, so often scoffed at by men and things, so often trampled by the fury of events and passions. I am not saying to you that it is an absolute certainty. There is no such thing in history as an absolute certainty. I know how many ailing spots are still in the joints of nations, from where a sudden, general, temporary inflammation can rise. But I also know that there are tendencies towards peace that are so strong, so deep, so essential, that it depends on you, through a conscious, deliberate, tireless will, to systematise these tendencies and to finally carry out the paradox of great human peace, as your fathers accomplished the paradox of great republican freedom. A difficult task, but not an impossible one.

The appeasement of prejudices and hatreds, always expanding alliances and federations, international economic and social conventions, international arbitration and simultaneous disarmament, the union of men in work and light: this, young people, will be the highest effort and glory of the rising generation. No, I am not proposing a disappointing dream. I am not proposing a weakening dream either. Let none of you believe that in the still difficult and uncertain period that will precede the definitive agreement of nations, we want to leave to the chance of our hopes, the smallest shred of France's security, dignity, and pride. Against all threats and all humiliation, it is necessary to defend it. It is doubly sacred to us, because it is France, and because it is human. Even the agreement of nations in definitive peace will not erase homelands, which will retain their profound historical originality, their own function in the common work of reconciled humanity. And if we do not want to wait to close the book of war, until force has put right all the iniquities committed by force, if we do not conceive of reparations as revenge, we know well that Europe, infused at last with the virtue and democracy and spirit of peace, will know how to find the conciliatory formulas that will free all the vanquished from the servitudes and distresses attached to conquest.

But firstly, and above all, we must break the circle of fatality, the circle of iron, the circle of hatred, where even just demands provoke reprisals that flatter themselves about being just, where war turns after war in a movement with no way out and no end, where right and violence, under the same bloody livery, are nearly no longer distinguishable from each other, and where torn humanity weeps for the victory of justice almost as much as for its defeat.

Above all, let no one accuse us of debasing, or provoking courage. Humanity is doomed if, in order to show courage, it is condemned to kill eternally. Courage, today, is not keeping the cloud of war hanging over the world, a terrible but dormant cloud about which we flatter ourselves by believing that it will only explode over others. Courage, is not leaving in the hands of force the solution to conflicts that reason can resolve, for courage is the exaltation of man, and this is its abdication. Courage, for all of you, at all times, is withstanding without relenting the tests of every kind, physical and moral, that life presents. Courage is not giving away your will to the random whims of impressions and forces. It is keeping up the habits of work and action in the inevitability of weariness. Courage in the infinite disorder of life, which calls us from all sides, is choosing a trade and doing it well, whatever it might be. It is not being put off by minute or monotonous detail. It is to become, as far as you can, an accomplished technician. It is accepting and understanding that the law of the specialisation of work is the condition of useful action, and yet allowing your eyes, your mind, a few sights of the wider world and perspectives. Courage is being altogether, and in whatever profession, both a practitioner and a philosopher. Courage is understanding one's own life, being more specific about it, going further into it, establishing it and nevertheless coordinating it with general life. Courage is keeping a close eye on your spinning and weaving machine, so that no thread breaks, and yet preparing for a wider and more fraternal social order in which the machine will be the common servant of liberated workers. Courage is accepting the new conditions that life makes in science and art, welcoming, exploring, the almost infinite complexity of facts and details, and yet illuminating this enormous and confused reality with general ideas, organising and uplifting it with the sacred beauty of forms and rhythms. Courage is controlling one's own faults, suffering for them, but not being overcome by them, and continuing on one's way. Courage is loving life and viewing death with a calm look. It is striving for the ideal and understanding the real. It is acting and giving oneself to great causes without knowing what reward the deep universe has reserved for our effort, nor whether it has any reward in store for us. Courage is seeking the truth and speaking it. It is about not submitting to the law of the triumphant passing lie, nor echoing, with our soul, mouth and hands, idiotic applause and fanatical booing.

Ah, really, how poor is our conception of life, how short-sighed our science of living, if we believe that with war abolished, men will lack opportunities to exercise and test their courage, and that we must prolong the drum rolls that in schools of the First French Empire made hearts jump! They sounded heroic then; in our twentieth century they would sound hollow. And you, young people, you want your lives to be alive, sincere and full. That is why I have told you, as I tell men, some of the things that I carry within me.

www.ingramcontent.com/pod-product-compliance
Lightning Source LLC
Chambersburg PA
CBHW070032030426
42335CB00017B/2397